EALRIS

13140005004311

World Languages

the library
IN EAST AYRSHIRE

D1470758

Please return item by last date sho
or renew either by phone
T: 01563 554300 or online at:
http://libcatalogue.east-ayrshire.gov.uk

CENTRAL

EDUCATION   RESOURCE   SERVICE

www.raintreepublishers.co.uk
Visit our website to find out
more information about
Raintree books.

To order:
☎ Phone 0845 6044371
🖨 Fax +44 (0) 1865 312263
💻 Email myorders@raintreepublishers.co.uk

Customers from outside the UK please telephone +44 1865 312262

Raintree is an imprint of Capstone Global Library Limited,
a company incorporated in England and Wales having its
registered office at 7 Pilgrim Street, London, EC4V 6LB
– Registered company number: 6695582

Text © Capstone Global Library Limited 2013
First published in hardback in 2013
First published in paperback in 2013
The moral rights of the proprietor have been asserted.

All rights reserved. No part of this publication may be reproduced in
any form or by any means (including photocopying or storing it in
any medium by electronic means and whether or not transiently or
incidentally to some other use of this publication) without the written
permission of the copyright owner, except in accordance with the
provisions of the Copyright, Designs and Patents Act 1988 or under
the terms of a licence issued by the Copyright Licensing Agency,
Saffron House, 6–10 Kirby Street, London EC1N 8TS (www.cla.co.uk).
Applications for the copyright owner's written permission should be
addressed to the publisher.

Edited by Daniel Nunn, Rebecca Rissman, and Sian Smith
Designed by Joanna Hinton-Malivoire
Picture research by Mica Brancic
Production by Alison Parsons
Originated by Capstone Global Library Ltd
Printed in China

ISBN 978 1 406 23921 8 (hardback)
16 15 14 13 12
10 9 8 7 6 5 4 3 2 1

ISBN 978 1 406 23928 7 (paperback)
17 16 15 14 13
10 9 8 7 6 5 4 3 2 1

British Library Cataloguing in Publication Data
Nunn, Daniel.
  Colours in Polish. -- (World languages. Colours)
  1. Polish language--Vocabulary--Juvenile literature.
  2. Colors--Juvenile literature. 3. Polish language--
  Textbooks for foreign speakers--English.
  I. Title II. Series
  491.8'582421-dc23

Acknowledgements
We would like to thank Shutterstock for permission to reproduce pho-
tographs: pp.4 (© Phiseksit), 5 (© Stephen Aaron Rees), 6 (© Tischenko
Irina), 7 (© Tony Magdaraog), 8 (© szefei), 9 (© Picsfive), 10 (© Eric
Isselée), 11 (© Yasonya), 12 (© Nadezhda Bolotina), 13 (© Maryna
Gviazdovska), 14 (© Erik Lam), 15 (© Eric Isselée), 16 (© Ruth Black),
17 (© blueskies9), 18 (© Alexander Dashewsky), 19 (© Michele
Perbellini), 20 (© Eric Isselée), 21 (© Roman Rvachov).

Cover photographs reproduced with permission of Shutterstock: dog
(© Erik Lam), strawberry (© Stephen Aaron Rees), fish (© Tischenko
Irina). Back cover photograph of a cat reproduced with permission of
Shutterstock (© Eric Isselée).

We would like to thank Dorota Holowiak for her invaluable assistance
in the preparation of this book.

Every effort has been made to contact copyright holders of
material reproduced in this book. Any omissions will be rectified in
subsequent printings if notice is given to the publisher.

Contents

Czerwony

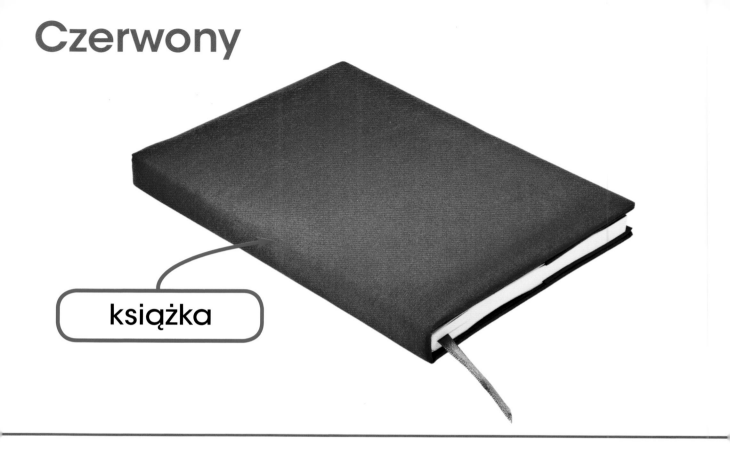

książka

Książka jest czerwona.

The book is red.

truskawka

Truskawka jest czerwona.

The strawberry is red.

Pomarańczowy

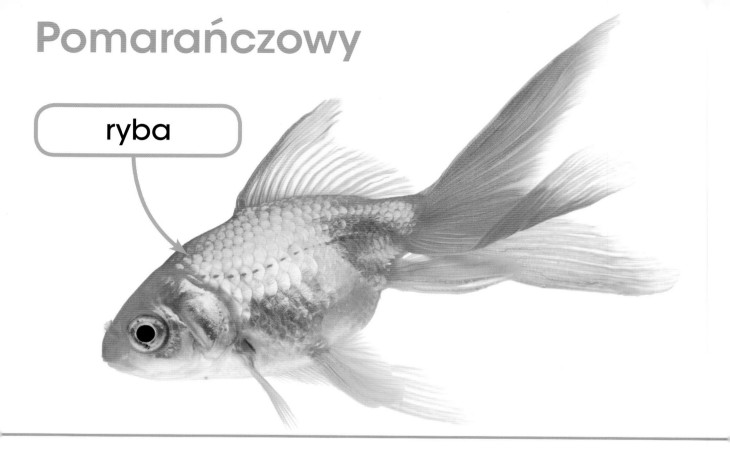

ryba

Ryba jest pomarańczowa.
The fish is orange.

marchewka

Marchewka jest pomarańczowa.

The carrot is orange.

Żółty

kwiat

Kwiat jest żółty.

The flower is yellow.

banan

Banan jest żółty.

The banana is yellow.

Zielony

ptak

Ptak jest zielony.

The bird is green.

jabłko

Jabłko jest zielone.

The apple is green.

Niebieski

T-shirt

T-shirt jest niebieski.

The T-shirt is blue.

kubek

Kubek jest niebieski.

The cup is blue.

Brązowy

pies

Pies jest brązowy.

The dog is brown.

krowa

Krowa jest brązowa.

The cow is brown.

Różowy

ciasto

Ciasto jest różowe.

The cake is pink.

kapelusz

Kapelusz jest różowy.

The hat is pink.

Biały

mleko

Mleko jest biało.

The milk is white.

śnieg

Śnieg jest biały.

The snow is white.

Czarny

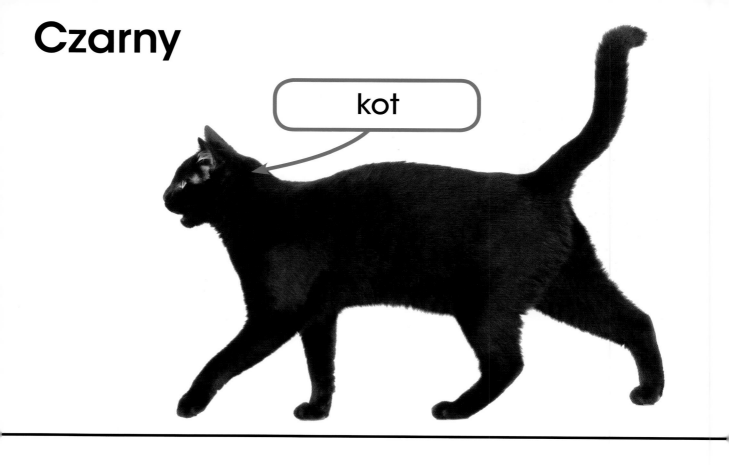

kot

Kot jest **czarny**.

The cat is **black**.

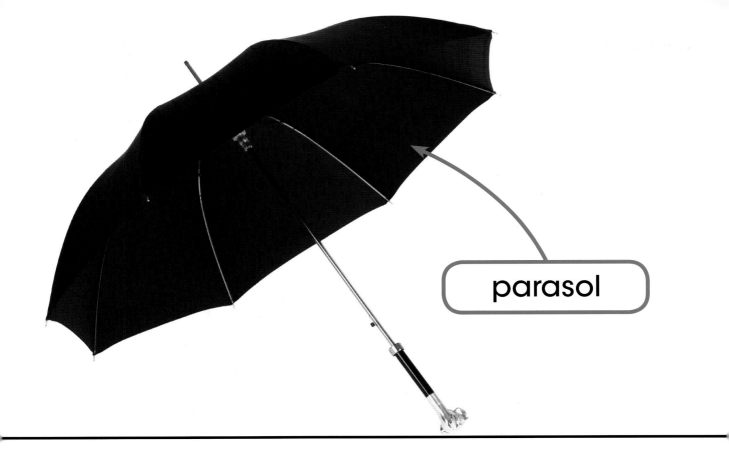

parasol

Parasol jest **czarny**.

The umbrella is **black**.

Dictionary

Polish word	How to say it	English word
banan	bah-nahn	banana
białe	bih-ah-veh	white
biały	bih-ah-vih	white
brązowa	brohn-zoh-vah	brown
brązowy	brohn-zoh-vih	brown
ciasto	chee-ah-stoh	cake
czarny	chahr-nih	black
czerwona	chehr-voh-nah	red
czerwony	chehr-voh-nih	red
jabłko	yah-b-koh	apple
jest	yeh-st	is
kapelusz	cup-el-oosh	hat
kot	cot	cat
krowa	cro-vah	cow
książka	ksee-ohn-sh-kah	book
kubek	coo-bek	cup
kwiat	cvee-aht	flower
marchewka	mahr-hev-kah	carrot

Polish word	How to say it	English word
mleko	mleh-koh	milk
niebieski	nee-e-bee-es-kih	blue
parasol	pah-rah-sohl	umbrella
pies	pee-ehs	dog
pomarańczowa	po-mah-rahn-cho-vah	orange
pomarańczowy	po-mah-rahn-cho-vih	orange
ptak	p-tahk	bird
różowe	roo-zho-vih	pink
różowy	roo-zho-vih	pink
ryba	rih-bah	fish
śnieg	sih-ni-ehg	snow
T-shirt	t-shirt	T-shirt
truskawka	troo-scuv-cah	strawberry
zielone	zee-eloh-neh	green
zielony	zee-eloh-nih	green
żółty	zhoov-tih	yellow

See words in the "How to say it" columns for a rough guide to pronunciations.

Index

Notes for parents and teachers

Polish does not use articles (for example, "the", "a", and "an"),
which is why there is no Polish word for "the". Polish nouns are either
feminine, masculine, or neuter, and the spelling of adjectives changes
according to the gender of the noun. This is why some of the colours in
Polish used in this book have more than one spelling.